FATWA ON S
BOMBINGS AND

TABLE OF CONTENT

&

BIBLIOGRAPHY

SHAYKH-UL-ISLAM
DR MUHAMMAD TAHIR-UL-QADRI

Translated by

Shaykh Abdul Aziz Dabbagh

Minhaj-ul-Quran International (UK)
292-296 Romford Road,
Forest Gate
London, E7 9HD
United Kingdom

www.minhaj.org | www.minhajuk.org | media.minhajuk.org

For Sales & Distribution Enquiries:
+44 (0) 208 257786

First Published in February 2010.

ISBN 10. 0955188849
ISBN 13. 9780955188848

Design & Typeset by MQI Publications
Printed in Great Britain by the MPG Books Group, Bodmin and King's Lynn

CONTENTS

FOREWORD

Presented here is the translation in English of the introduction, together with the contents listing and bibliography, of the fatwa, or Islamic decree, delivered by His Eminence Shaykh-ul-Islam Dr Muhammad Tahir-ul-Qadri, a highly renowned Islamic scholar and recognised authority on Islam, on the vital matter of suicide bombings and terrorist attacks carried out in the name of Islam. It is regarded as a significant and historic step, the first time that such an explicit and unequivocal decree against the perpetrators of terror has been broadcast so widely.

The original fatwa has been written in Urdu, and amounts to 600 pages of research and references from the Qur'an, Hadith [traditions and sayings of the Prophet Muhammad (s)], opinions of the Companions (of the Prophet), and the widely accepted classical texts of Islamic scholarship. The introduction presented here is intended to provide the general reader with the essential message of the decree, while the table of contents is fleshed out to provide a foretaste of the relevant topics discussed and elucidated in the full version, which will eventually be translated fully into English. The bibliography is provided at the end of this English translation in order to detail the numerous texts referred to by the author. The comprehensiveness and extent of the original work is meant to leave no doubt, and leave no stone unturned, in order to remove any possible justification for the suicide attacks that the perpetrators or their supporters may offer. Indeed, Dr Tahir-ul-Qadri goes that crucial step forward and announces categorically that suicide bombings and attacks against civilian targets are not only condemned by Islam, but render the perpetrators totally out of the fold of Islam, in other words, to be unbelievers. Furthermore, in what is unprecedented in recent Islamic scholarship, this work draws out scriptural, historical, and classical scholarly references highlighting the obligations of Governments of Islamic nations to deal decisively to root out terrorist elements from society.

The fatwa has been delivered in the context mainly of the recent spate of suicide atrocities carried out in Pakistan against a variety of civilian targets. Nonetheless, there are clear verdicts within the fatwa that apply, with no less vigour, to attacks carried out against Western targets in Muslim countries, or indeed in the West itself, by so-called home-grown terrorists.

It is hoped that this work will have a profound impact on two main counts. Firstly, it will dispense with the notion that Islam and Muslims are somehow synonymous with terrorism, and remove the charge levelled against Muslims, and their scholars in particular, that they do not do enough to condemn terrorist attacks. Secondly, and more crucially, this decree will provide clear, categorical and comprehensive injunctions that will dissuade the confused and impressionable young Muslims, whether in the East or West, from embarking upon the path of extremism and radicalism that eventually leads to the deadly and horrific outcomes we have all tragically come to know.

Dr Zahid Iqbal
Editor of English version

TABLE OF CONTENTS

1. The dignity of a believer is greater than that of the Ka'ba
2. Merely pointing a weapon towards a believer is prohibited
3. The forbiddance of the mass killing of Muslims and violence
4. The prohibition of killing someone accepting *Islām* while fighting
5. Becoming an accomplice to terrorists is also a crime
6. Those attacking mosques are the greatest wrongdoers

SECTION 2
THE PUNISHMENT FOR TORTURING AND KILLING MUSLIMS

1. Killing a Muslim is a greater sin than destroying the whole world
2. Killing a human is like disbelieving
3. The massacre of Muslims is a blasphemous act
4. Like polytheism, murder too is the greatest wrong
5. Bloodshed is the greatest of all crimes

6. Those burning the Muslims by explosions and other means belong to Hell
7. Those burning the Muslims are debarred from the fold of *Islām*
8. No act of worship by the murderer of a Muslim is acceptable
9. Those who torture the Muslims will face the torment of Hell

SECTION 3
SUICIDE IS A FORBIDDEN ACT

1. The forbiddance and prohibition of suicide
2. Paradise is forbidden to the one who commits suicide
3. The gist of the discussion

CHAPTER 3
THE FORBIDDANCE OF THE INDISCRIMINATE KILLING OF NON-MUSLIMS AND OF TORTURING THEM.

1. Killing the non-Muslim citizens is forbidden
2. The forbiddance of killing foreign delegates and religious leaders

3. Retribution of Muslims and non-Muslims is the same
4. Avenging a wrong done by a non-Muslim to others is forbidden
5. The forbiddance of looting non-Muslim citizens
6. Humiliating non-Muslim citizens is forbidden
7. The protection of non-Muslim citizens from internal and external aggression

CHAPTER 4

THE FORBIDDANCE OF TERRORISM AGAINST THE NON-MUSLIMS EVEN DURING WAR

1. The prohibition of the killing of non-Muslim women
2. The prohibition of the killing of the children of non-Muslims
3. The prohibition of the killing of the aged non-Muslims
4. The prohibition of the killing of non-Muslim religious leaders
5. The prohibition of the killing of non-Muslim traders and farmers

6. The prohibition of the killing of non-Muslim service personnel
7. The prohibition of the killing of non-Muslim non-combatants
8. Night offensives against non-Muslims is prohibited
9. The burning of the inhabitants of non-Muslim war areas is prohibited
10. Breaking into the enemy houses and looting them is forbidden
11. Damaging the cattle, crops and properties of the enemy is forbidden

CHAPTER 5

THE PROTECTION OF THE NON-MUSLIMS' LIVES, PROPERTIES AND PLACES OF WORSHIP

SECTION 1

THE PROTECTION OF NON-MUSLIM CITIZENS DURING THE PROPHETIC PERIOD AND THE ERA OF THE RIGHTLY GUIDED CALIPHS

1. The protection of non-Muslim citizens in the days of the Holy Prophet (blessings and peace be upon him)

2. The legal status of the protection of non-Muslims in the days of Abū Bakr Ṣiddīq
3. The legal status of the protection of non-Muslims in the days of ʻUmar
4. The legal status of the protection of non-Muslims in the days of ʻUthmān
5. The legal status of the protection of non-Muslims in the days of ʻAlī
6. The legal status of the protection of non-Muslims in the days of ʻUmar ibn ʻAbd al-ʻAzīz

Section 2
The Forbiddance of Enforcing One's Beliefs and Annihilating Places of Worship

1. The complete freedom of holding fast to one's religion and its practice
2. Killing a non-Muslim and destroying his property due to religious differences is forbidden
3. Safeguarding the non-Muslims' places of worship is a practice of the Holy Prophet
4. Safeguarding the non-Muslims' places of worship is obligatory

5. The annihilation of the non-Muslims' places of worship located in Muslim-majority areas is prohibited

SECTION 3
RULES CONCERNING THE BASIC RIGHTS OF THE NON-MUSLIM CITIZENS IN AN ISLAMIC STATE

CHAPTER 6

REBELLION AGAINST THE MUSLIM STATE, ADMINISTRATION AND GOVERNANCE IS FORBIDDEN

SECTION 1
WHAT IS REBELLION AND WHO IS A REBEL?
(TERMINOLOGY, DEFINITIONS AND SIGNS)

1. The lexical definition of rebellion
2. The technical definition of rebellion
    i. Rebellion according to the Ḥanafī school of thought
    ii. Rebellion according to the Mālikī jurists
    iii. Shafi'ī's definition of rebellion

SECTION 2

THE GRAVITY OF THE CRIME OF REBELLION AND ITS PUNISHMENT

Section 3
The Legal Status of Killings against a Corrupt Government

1. The forbiddance of rebellion against a government that is not explicitly idolatrous
2. Raising arms against Muslims is an idolatrous act
3. The legal and constitutional way of changing a corrupt government

Section 4
Decrees of the Four Imāms and Other Eminent Authorities of the *Umma* against Terrorism and Rebellion

1. The decree of Imām A'zam Abū Ḥanīfa about fighting against the terrorists
2. The decree of Imām Mālik against the terrorists
3. The decree of Imām Shafi'ī against the terrorist rebels
4. The action and decree of Imām Aḥmad ibn Ḥanbal against mutiny
5. The decree of Imām Sufyān Thawrī about rebellion
6. Imām Ṭaḥawī's decree against armed rebellion

Section 5
Decrees by contemporary Salafi scholars against rebels

2. Declaring Muslims to be disbelievers is a sign of the Khawārij: Shaykh 'Abdu'llāh ibn Bāz
3. The terrorists of today are a gang of the ignorant: Shaykh Ṣāliḥ al-Fawzān
4. Terrorist activities are not *Jihād*: Muftī Nazīr Ḥusayn of Delhi
5. The gist of the discussion

CHAPTER 7

THE KHAWĀRIJ STRIFE AND CONTEMPORARY TERRORISTS

SECTION 1

THE ADVENT OF THE KHAWĀRIJ STRIFE AND THEIR BELIEFS AND IDEOLOGIES

1. Lexical and technical meanings
2. The Khawārij strife in the light of the Holy Qur'ān
3. The advent of the Khawārij disruption in the days of the Holy Prophet
4. The ideological development of the Khawārij disruption in the period of 'Uthmān
5. The start of the Khawārij as a movement in the 'Alawī period

6. The beliefs and ideologies of the Khawārij
7. The psychology and mental attributes of the Khawārij
8. How the Khawārij would rouse religious sentiments for persuasion
9. The conspicuous innovations of the Khawārij
10. The research work of Imām Abū Bakr al-Ājurrī

SECTION 2
THE SAYINGS OF THE MESSENGER OF ALLAH ABOUT THE KHAWĀRIJ TERRORISTS

1. The terrorists would appear religious
2. The Khawārij slogans would seem true to the common man
3. The Khawārij would use adolescents for terrorist activities after brainwashing
4. The Khawārij would appear from the East
5. The Khwarij would keep coming until the time of False Messiah
6. The Khawārij will be absolutely debarred from the fold of *Islām*

7. The Khawārij will be the dogs of Hell
8. The religious appearance of the Khawārij must not be mistaken
9. The Khawārij are the worst of creation
10. A noteworthy point
11. The saying of the Holy Prophet: The decree to eliminate the Khawārij strife
    i. The total elimination of the Khawārij is mandatory
    ii. Important expositions of the ḥadīth Imāms
    iii. The underlying reason for the comparsion with the people of 'Ad and Thamūd for the elimination of the Khawārij
    iv. The great reward for eliminating the Khawārij
    v. The signs of the Khawārij terrorists – a collective picture

SECTION 3

THE EXPOSITIONS OF THE IMĀMS ON THE MANDATORY ELIMINATION OF THE KHAWĀRIJ AND DECLARING THEM DISBELIEVERS

The decrees of the Imāms on two known statements about declaring the Khawārij as disbelievers

The first statement: the application of the decree of disbelief to the Khawārij

1. Imām al-Bukhārī (256 AH)
2. Imām Ibn Jarīr aṭ-Ṭabarī (310 AH)
3. Imām Muḥammad ibn Muḥammad al-Ghazālī (505 AH)
4. Qāḍī Abū Bakr ibn al-'Arabī (543 AH)
5. Qāḍī 'Iyāḍ al-Mālikī (544 AH)
6. Imām Abu'l-'Abbās al-Qurṭubī (656 AH)
7. 'Allāma Ibn Taymiyya (728 AH)
8. Imām Taqī ad-Dīn as-Subkī (756 AH)
9. Imām Shāṭibī al-Mālikī (790 AH)
10. Imām Ibn al-Bazzāz al-Kurdarī al-Ḥanafī (827 AH)
11. Imām Badr ad-Dīn al-'Ainī al-Ḥanafī (855 AH)
12. Imām Aḥmad bin Muḥammad al-Qasṭalānī (923 AH)
13. Mullā 'Alī al-Qārī (1014 AH)
14. Shaykh 'Abd al-Ḥaqq Muḥaddith of Dehli (1052 AH)
15. Shāh 'Abd al-'Azīz Muḥaddith of Dehli (1229 AH)

16. ‘Allāma Ibn ‘Abidīn Shāmī (1306 AH)
17. ‘Allāma ‘Abd ar-Raḥmān Mubārakpūrī (1353 AH)

The second statement: the application of the decree of rebellion to the Khawārij

1. Imām A‘zam Abū Ḥanīfa (150 AH)
2. Imām Shams ad-Dīn as-Sarkhasī (483 AH)
3. Hafiẓ Ibn Ḥajar al-‘Asqalānī (852 AH)
4. Imām Aḥmad Raḍā Khān (1340 AH)

Reasons of the ḥadīth Imāms about consensus on eliminating the Khawārij

1. Qāḍī ‘Iyāḍ al-Mālikī (544 AH)
2. ‘Allāma Ibn Taymiyya (728 AH)
3. Hafiẓ Ibn Ḥajar al-‘Asqalānī (728 AH)

The great reward for the troops fighting against the Khawārij terrorists

1. Ibn Habīrah

The standpoint of 'Allāma Anwar Shāh Kashmīrī and 'Allāma Shabbīr Aḥmad 'Uthmānī about the Khawārij

SECTION 4

TODAY'S TERRORISTS ARE THE KHAWĀRIJ

1. Condemnation of the supporters of the Khawārij
2. Research work by Ibn Taymiyya about the perpetuation of the Khawārij
3. The terrorists are the Khawārij of our times
4. An important juristic issue: labelling the Khawārij terrorists is based on the Qur'ān and *Sunna*, not independent reasoning

CHAPTER 8

THE PEACEFUL WAY OF STRUGGLE IN A MUSLIM STATE

1. The Qur'ānic command to bid good and forbid evil
2. The collective struggle for commanding good and forbidding evil
3. The command to bid good and forbid evil in Prophetic traditions
4. The three grades of preventing evil

CHAPTER 9

CALL FOR REFLECTION AND REFORMATION

SUMMARY OF FATWA

The horrendous onslaught of terrorist activity that has continued unabated for the last many years has brought the Muslim Umma, and Pakistan in particular, into disrepute. There is no denying the fact that the vast majority of Muslims oppose and condemn terrorism in unequivocal terms and are not ready to accept it as even remotely related to Islam in any manner. However, a negligible minority amongst them seems to give terrorism tacit approval. Instead of openly opposing and condemning terrorism, these people confuse the entire subject by resorting to misleading and perplexing discussions.

It may be true that among the fundamental local, national and international factors underpinning terrorism on a global level include: the injustices being currently meted out to the Muslims in certain matters, the apparent double standards displayed by the main powers, and their open-ended and long-term military engagements in a number of countries under the pretext of eliminating terror. But the terrorists' recourse to violent and indiscriminate killings have become a routine affair, taking the form of suicide bombings against innocent and peaceful people, bomb blasts on mosques, shrines, educational institutions, bazaars, governmental buildings, trade centres, markets, security installations, and other public places: heinous, anti-human and barbarous acts in their very essence. These people justify their actions of human destruction and mass killing of innocent people in the name of Jihad (holy struggle against evil) and thus distort, twist and confuse the entire Islamic concept of Jihad. This situation is causing Muslims, the young in particular, to fall prey to doubts and reservations, muddling their minds in respect of Jihad, because those perpetrating these atrocities are from amongst the Muslims. The perpetrators practice Islamic rituals, perform acts of worship and put on outward forms set down in Sharia. This has put not only the common Muslims into a dilemma, but also a significant number of religious scholars and intellectuals, who are disconcerted and curious to know truly the exact and precise Islamic injunctions underpinning the workings, methods and measures these individuals and groups have adopted to cause their havoc.

Furthermore, the Western media is wont of over-reporting incidents of terrorism and extremism around the Muslim world, and does not at all highlight the positive and constructive aspects of Islam, its peaceful teachings and philanthropic philosophy and orientation. Moreover, it does not report the abhorrence, condemnation and opposition prevalent within Muslim communities towards extremists, militants and terrorists. Bracketing both Islam and terrorism together has led only to negative consequences. The western mind conjures up images of terrorism and extremism at the merest mention of the word 'Islam', leaving Western-bred and educated Muslim youth in a most difficult position, and leaving them ever more puzzled. In fact, the present generation of young Muslims all over the Islamic world is falling victim to intellectual confusion, as well as deterioration in the practical fields and in the domain of beliefs and religious tenets.

Because of this situation, two kinds of negative response and destructive attitude are developing: one in the form of damage to Islam and the Muslim world, and the other a threat to humanity, and the Western world in particular. The damage to Islam and the Muslim world is that Muslim youth, not completely and comprehensively aware of Islamic teachings, and under the influence of the media, regard terrorism and extremism as emanating from religious teachings and attitudes of religious people. This misplaced thinking is alienated them from religion, leading them to atheism, and posing a serious danger to the Muslim Umma in future. On the other hand, the danger threatening the Western world and humanity is of the above-mentioned policies and stereotyping of Muslims provoking a negative response among some of the Muslim youth, who regard these attacks against Islam as an organised conspiracy from certain influential circles in the western world. By way of reaction, they are gradually becoming extreme and militant in their outlook, departing moderation and a poised outlook on life, and, charged with hatred and revenge, ultimately becoming terrorists, or at the very least being groomed into the extremists' designs. Thus, Western policies are instrumental in producing and inducting potential terrorist recruits and supporters, with no end in sight. In consequence, both the Muslim Umma, as well as humanity, is heading towards catastrophe.

Moreover, these circumstances are heightening tension, and creating an increasingly large deficit of trust between the Islamic and the Western worlds. The upsurge in terrorism is paving the way for greater foreign interference in and pressure on the Muslim states. This widening gulf is not only pushing humanity towards inter-faith antagonism at the global level but also reducing totally the possibilities of peace, tolerance and mutual coexistence among the different human societies of the world.

We thought it necessary, under these circumstances, to place the Islamic stance on terrorism precisely in its proper perspective before the Western and Islamic worlds, in the light of the Holy Qur'an, Prophetic traditions and Books of Jurisprudence and Belief. We want to put across this point of view before all the significant institutions, important think tanks and influential opinion-making organisations in the world so that both the Muslims and non-Muslims , entertaining doubts and reservations about Islam, are enabled to understand Islam's standpoint on terrorism more clearly and unambiguously. The contents of this research work are summarized here briefly.

The first chapter of this document, explaining and elaborating the meaning of Islam, discusses its three categories i.e. Islam (peace), Iman (faith) and Ihsan (spiritual excellence). These three words, literally and metaphorically, collectively represent peace, safety, mercy, tolerance, forbearance, love, kindness, benevolence and respect for humanity.

It has been proven in the second chapter of this document through dozens of Qur'anic verses and Prophetic traditions that the killing of Muslims and the perpetration of terrorism are not only unlawful and forbidden in Islam but also represent the rejection of faith. Through reference to the expositions and opinions of jurists and experts of exegeses and Hadith, it has been established that all the learned authorities have held the same opinion about terrorism in the 1400 year history of Islam.

The third chapter of this work describes the rights of non-Muslim citizens quite comprehensively. The opinions of all the leading jurists in this regard have also been listed in the light of various Qur'anic verses and Prophetic traditions.

In addition to all this, the most important point this research study has undertaken to make revolves around the thought, ideology and mindset, which pits a Muslim against another and finally leads him to massacre innocent humans. Such a mindset not only regards the killing of women shopping in markets and schoolgirls permissible but also a means of earning rewards and spiritual benefits. What power or conviction rouses him to kill people gathered in the mosque, and earn Paradise through carnage? Why does a terrorist decide to end his own life, the greatest blessing of Allah Almighty, with his own hands through suicide bombings? How does he come to believe that by killing innocent people through suicide bombing he would become a martyr and enter

Paradise? These are the questions that spring to the mind of every person possessing common sense. While furnishing befitting answers to these questions, we have relied on historical facts, besides scholarly arguments, which the Holy Prophet (blessings and peace be upon him) himself predicted. By undertaking a comprehensive analysis of the signs, beliefs and ideologies of the Khawarij through the Qur'anic verses, Prophetic traditions and jurisprudential opinions of jurists, we have established that the terrorists are the Khawarij of contemporary times.

After declaring terrorism as forbidden, and an act of rebellion and brutality, and indeed of infidelity, we have drawn the attention of all the responsible powers and stakeholders to the topic "Call to Reflect and Reform", to the need for eliminating all the factors that cause people to entertain doubts, and reinforce the hidden hands actively engaged in spreading the plague of terrorism. A notable theme under discussion these days is that since foreign powers are causing unwarranted and unjustified interference in Muslim countries, including Pakistan, the so-called Jihadi groups have thwarted them by launching the offensive, inflicting upon them devastating blows and that their actions, though not right and justifiable, should not be reviled and condemned because their intention is to defend Islam. In our view, this is an awful witticism and a most deplorable stance. To remove this misconception, we have specified a brief portion of the treatise, in the beginning, to this subject, bringing to the fore the fact that, in the light of the Qur'an and Hadith, evil cannot become good under any circumstances, nor can oppression transform itself into virtuous deed due to goodness of intention.

After these explanatory submissions, we also regard it our fundamental duty to let everyone know without any grain of doubt that we are going ahead with the publication of this research work solely for the sake of the respect and dignity of Islam and in the service of humanity. We do not mean to condone or approve the unpopular and unwise policies of global powers through this edict, nor do we aim to justify the wrong policies of any government, including that of Pakistan. We neither seek the pleasure of any government, nor tribute or appreciation from any international power or organisation. As always, we have taken the initiative to perform this task as a part of our religious obligation. Our objective in doing so is to wash off the stain of terrorism from the fair face of Islam, to familiarise the Muslims with the real teachings of the

Holy Qur'an and Sunna and attempt to rid humanity suffering from the raging fire of terrorism.

May Almighty Allah bless this endeavour with His benevolent acceptance through the holy means of His Beloved Messenger (blessings and peace be upon him).

THE QUESTIONS THAT SPRING TO MIND AND THEIR BRIEF ANSWERS

The heartbreakingly gory scenes of terrorism will no doubt disturb the minds of all eminent and common people of the world with some perplexing questions that demand satisfactory answers. We have attempted to supply detailed, logical and matter-of-fact replies to these inquiries. Brief answers to these questions are appended here in sequence, while their details have been presented in the same order in subsequent chapters of this research work.

1. Q: The first question in this connection that concerns all relates to use of force to spread beliefs: is it lawful for a group or organisation to use force to promote and put into effect their own creed and beliefs in the name of reforming others' beliefs and ideologies, presuming themselves to be on the right path? Does Islam allow, somehow, the killing of people because of ideological differences, looting their wealth

and properties and destroying mosques, religious places and shrines?

- A: Islam is a religion of peace and safety that champions love and harmony in society. According to Islamic teachings, only such a person will be called a Muslim at whose hands the lives and properties of all innocent Muslims and non-Muslims remain safe and unhurt. The sanctity of human life and its protection occupies a fundamental place in Islamic law. Taking anyone's life for nothing is an act that is forbidden and unlawful. Rather, in some cases, it amounts to infidelity. These days, the terrorists, in a vain attempt to impose their own ideas and beliefs and eliminate their opponents from the face of the earth, killing innocent people ruthlessly and indiscriminately everywhere in mosques, bazaars, governmental offices and other public places are in fact committing clear infidelity. They are warned of humiliating torment in this world and in the hereafter. Terrorism, in its very essence, is an act that symbolises infidelity and rejection of what Islam stands for. When the forbidden element of suicide is added to it, its severity and gravity becomes even greater. Scores of Qur'anic verses and Prophetic traditions have proved that the massacre of Muslims and terrorism is unlawful in

Islam; rather, they are blasphemous acts. This has always been the opinion unanimously held by all the scholars that have passed in the 1400 years of Islamic history, including all the eminent Imams of Tafseer and Hadith and authorities on logic and jurisprudence. Islam has kept the door of negotiation and discussion open to convince by reasoning, instead of the taking up of arms to declare the standpoint of others as wrong, and enforcing one's own opinion. Only the victims of ignorance, jealousy and malice go for militancy. Islam declares them rebels. They will abide in Hell.

2. Q: The second question in this regard is: what are the rights of the non-Muslim citizens in a Muslim state?

- A: Islam not only guarantees the protection of life, honour and property of Muslim citizens of an Islamic state, but also assures the equal protection of life, honour and property of non-Muslim citizens and of those people too with whom it has entered into a peace treaty. The rights of non-Muslim citizens enjoy the same sanctity as those of Muslim citizens in an Islamic state. There is no difference between them as human beings. That is why Islamic law metes out equal treatment to both Muslims and non-Muslims in the matters of blood money and Qisas. Non-Muslims have complete personal and religious freedom in a Muslim society. Their properties and places of worship also enjoy complete protection. Besides non-Muslim citizens, even the ambassadors of non-Muslim countries and others working on diplomatic assignments have been guaranteed complete protection. Likewise, the protection of life and property of non-Muslim traders is the responsibility of the Islamic state. Islam does not allow and advocate the use of violence against and killing of peaceful and non-combatant citizens under any circumstances. Those indulging in attacks on peaceful non-Muslim citizens, kidnapping them for ransom, and torturing them mentally or physically, or keeping them under unlawful custody, are in fact committing serious violations of Islamic teachings.

3. Q: The third question arises: does Islam offer clear commands on the sanctity of human life? Is it lawful to kidnap and assassinate foreign delegates and innocent and peaceful non-Muslim citizens to avenge the injustices and disruption of the non-Muslim global powers?

- A: The importance Islam lays on the sanctity and dignity of human life can be gauged from the fact that Islam does not allow indiscriminate killing even when Muslim armies are engaged in war against enemy troops. The killing of children, women, the old, infirm, religious leaders and traders is strictly prohibited. Nor can those who surrender their arms, confine themselves to their homes and seek shelter of anyone be killed. The public cannot be massacred. Likewise, places of worship, buildings, crops and even trees cannot be destroyed. On the one hand, there is a clear set of Islamic laws based on extreme discretion, and on the other, there are people who invoke the name of Islam to justify the indiscriminate killing of people, children, and women everywhere, without any distinction of religion or identity. It is a pity that such barbaric people still refer to their activities as Jihad. There can be no bigger discrepancy than this to be seen on earth. It can in no way be permissible to keep foreign delegates under unlawful custody and murder them and other peaceful non-Muslim citizens in retaliation for the interference, unjust activities and aggressive advances of their countries. The one who does has no relation to Islam and the Holy Prophet (blessings and peace be upon him).

4. Q: The fourth and very significant question concerns rebellion: is armed struggle permissible against Muslim rulers to remove their governments because of their non-Islamic policies, or for the acceptance of demands, to bring them to the right path, or get them to give up their impious activities? Is rebellion permissible against the constitutional government, its writ and governance? What should be the legitimate way to change the rulers or make them mend their ways?

- A: Islam is not merely a religion. It is a complete *Deen*, a code of life. Providing a complete set of principles for every walk of life, it has also made arrangements for the protection of the collectivity of society. The rights and duties of state institutions have manifestly and clearly been spelled out. All citizens of the Muslim state have been placed under obligation to abide by state laws, rules and regulations. One of these principles is that a Muslim state and society should be a paragon of peace and mutual coexistence. That is why Islam strictly prohibits the taking up of arms against a Muslim state, to challenge its authority and writ, and declare war against it. Islamic law holds such an action as rebellion. God forbid if such conditions are created, then it is the primary responsibility of an

Islamic state to take urgent measures to eliminate rebellion with an iron hand and exterminate terrorism so that no individual or group can dare destroy the social harmony of society, ruin peace and shed innocent blood. Islam holds the peace and tranquillity of society in general, and of a Muslim state in particular, so dear that it does not allow people to raise the banner of revolt in the name of tackling injustice, oppression and other vices of the ruling elite. In the light of Prophetic traditions, the banner of rebellion against a Muslim state cannot be raised unless the rulers commit explicit, declared and absolute infidelity, and prevent the performance of religious rituals like prayer through the use of force.

The conditions leading to the forbiddance of rebellion in the light of the Qur'anic verses, Prophetic traditions and expositions of the jurists are evident. Referring to the holy Companions, their successors, Imam Abu Hanifa, Imam Malik, Imam Shafai, Imam Ahmad Bin Hanbal and other leading jurists, the fact has been brought to light that absolute consensus exists among all the leading jurists on the total forbiddance of rebellion against the Muslim state, and there is no difference of opinion between any schools of thought. Such a rebellion as challenges the writ of the state, and has been launched without the collective approval and sanction of society, is but a civil war, blatant terrorism and a clear act of strife. It can never be called Jihad under any circumstances.

As for the struggle to reform some impious Muslim ruler or state, that is not at all prohibited or disallowed. The forbiddance of rebellion and armed struggle should not mean at all that an evil should not be called an evil and no effort be made to stop its spread, or the obligation of faith to bid good and forbid evil be abandoned. Certification of truth and rejection of falsehood is binding upon Muslims. Likewise, seeking to reform society and fight off evil forces is one of the religious obligations. The adoption of all constitutional, legal, political and democratic ways to reform the rulers and the system of governance, and stop them from the violation of human rights is not only lawful but also binding upon Muslims. Making efforts at the individual and collective levels to establish truth, and ending the reign of terror and oppression and restoration of a system of justice through appropriate means form part of the obligations of faith.

5. Q: The sect of the Khawarij is etched into the history of terrorism. The question arises: who were the Khawarij? What does the Islamic law ordain about

them? Are the present day terrorists a continuation of the Khawarij?

- A: The Khawarij were rebels and apostates of Islam. Their advent took place during the period of the Prophet Muhammad (blessings and peace be upon him). Their intellectual growth and organised emergence took place during the Caliphates of Usman (ra) and Ali (ra). The Khawarij were so punctual and regular in the performance of religious rituals and acts of worship that they would appear more pious than the holy Companions would at times. However, in keeping with the clear command of the Holy Prophet (blessings and peace be upon him), they were absolutely out of the fold of Islam. The Khawarij would regard the killing of Muslims as lawful, reject the Companions for their disagreement with them, and, raising the slogan 'there is no Command but Allah's', consider the launch of armed struggle against and the killing of Hazrat Ali (ra) as lawful. They would continue in perpetrating these heinous actions. The Khawarij were in fact the first terrorist and rebellious group that challenged the writ of the state and raised the banner of armed struggle against a Muslim state. The texts of Hadith clearly establish that such elements would continue to be born in every age. The term

Khawarij is not meant merely to denote the group which took up arms against the rightly guided Caliphs, but it encompasses all those groups and individuals bearing such attributes, ideologies and terrorist ways of action who will continue to rear their head and perpetrate terrorism in the name of Jihad till the Day of Judgment. Despite being almost perfectionist in the performance of outward religious rituals, they would be considered as being out of the fold of Islam for their mistaken and misplaced ideology. A Muslim state cannot be allowed to give them any concession in the name of dialogue or stop military action without their complete elimination according to the explicit instructions of the Holy Prophet (blessings and peace be upon him). The only exception as to when they can be spared is that they lay down their arms, repent of their actions and vow to honour the state laws and writ of the Muslim state.

6. Q: What are the measures that the government and the ruling classes should take to put an end to mischief-mongering, terrorist activities and armed strife?

- A: The government and the law enforcing agencies should, at the outset, remove all factors and stimuli that contribute to making the common man a victim of doubt. Due to these factors, the ringleaders and the chieftains of terrorism are able to snare impressionable young people into changing their track and lead them to militancy. Exploiting their sentiments, they are able to prepare them for terrorist activities without much difficulty. The policies, events and circumstances the terrorist elements use as fuel for their evil agenda need to be remedied and set right as a priority. This will certainly help eradicate the root causes of the spread of this plague. Similarly, as long as the world powers, along with the Pakistani agencies, continue to neglect attending to the real hardships of people, removing their complaints and abandoning their deceptive policies, the restoration of real peace will remain merely a dream.

7. Q: Another important question under inquiry in various circles of society refers to a dilemma: can we justify as lawful the atrocities of terrorism if they are done with the intention of promoting Islam and to secure the rights of the Muslims?

- A: The Khawarij, even today, invoke Islam and raise slogans to establish the Divine Order, but all of their actions and steps constitute a clear violation of Islamic teachings. When their supporters do not have any legal argument to defend the actions of the Khawarij, they draw the attention of people to the vices of the ruling elites and the oppression by foreign forces as a justification for their killing. They are content in the belief that although the terrorists are doing wrong, their intention is good beyond any doubt. This is a major intellectual *faux pas* and many people, both educated and uneducated, suffer from this doubt. An evil act remains evil in all its forms and content; whatever we may interpret as injustice, this principle remains the same. Therefore, no forbidden action can ever become a virtuous and lawful deed due to goodness of intention. Law in Islam applies to an action. The massacre of humanity, perpetration of oppression and cruelty, terrorism, violence and bloodshed on earth and armed rebellion and strife cannot become pardonable actions due to any good intention or pious conviction. Nor is there any place for deviation from this fundamental principle. Thus, this argument of the terrorists and their well-wishers is also false in the sight of Islamic law. Therefore, we begin our arguments with the clarification of the same issue that an evil deed cannot change into a pious deed due to any pious intention it supposedly arises from.

GOOD INTENTION CAN NEVER CHANGE A VICE INTO VIRTUE

If a good intention gives rise to bloodshed and massacre, the question arises whether such tyranny and barbarism can be declared lawful on this basis. Some people think that although suicide explosions are atrociously evil, and that killing innocent people too is a monstrous crime, and spreading mischief and strife in the country is, again, a heinous act, while the destruction of educational, training, industrial, commercial and welfare centres and institutions is still a greater sin, the suicide bombers are doing this with good intention and pious motive. Therefore, they are justified. They are retaliating against foreign aggression against Muslims. They are carrying out a Jihad, and so, they cannot be given any blame.

In this brief discussion, we shall analyse this thought in the light of the Qur'an and Sunna. The Qur'an rejected as disbelief the idol-worship that was carried out with the intention of attaining the nearness of Allah. We find a detailed account of this matter in the Qur'an and Sunna. Some of the holy verses are produced here to facilitate comprehension of the issue.

The Qur'an says:

> *"(Say to the people:) 'Listen, sincere obedience and worship is only Allāh's due. And those (disbelievers) who have taken (idols as) helpers other than Allāh (say in false justification of their idol-worship:) 'We worship them only that they may bring us near to Allāh.' Surely, Allāh will judge between them concerning the matter in which they differ. Certainly Allāh does not give him guidance who is a liar, very ungrateful."*
>
> (Al-Qur'an, 39-3)

When the idolaters of Makka were asked the reason for idol-worship, they said the idols would bring them into Allah's proximity. The intention to attain Allah's nearness is good, but idol-worship is blasphemy and disbelief. Idolatry, therefore, cannot be justified because of good intention.

Similarly, the terrorists' claim of reformation too cannot be accepted because, through their actions, they demonstrate bloodshed and violence instead of constructive work and reformation. Allah Most High says:

> *"And among people there is also someone whose conversation seems to you pleasing in the life of the world and who calls Allāh to witness that which is in his heart, but in truth he is most quarrelsome. And when he turns away (from you), he runs about in the land to do (everything possible) to rouse mischief and destroy crops and life. And Allāh does not like mischief and violence. And when it is said to him (on account of this tyranny and violence): 'Fear Allāh,' his arrogance stimulates him for more sins. Hell is, therefore, sufficient for him. And that is indeed an evil abode."*
>
> (Al-Qur'an, 204-206)

These verses too describe that many people will make conversation, appearing pleasant in the arena of superficial arguments. They will swear on their good intentions, and declare Allah witness to their noble objectives and pious aims. Despite their assertions and testimonial claims, however, Allah has declared them miscreants and evil-mongers to face the torment of Hell. So their swearing on their intentions has been refuted because they are committing sheer acts of violence, strife and terrorism. Their crimes, therefore, cannot be forgiven due to their 'good' intentions and noble designs declared on oath. This is the basic principle drawn from the Qur'an and Islamic Law.

These Qur'anic verses explain the same point:

> *"When it is said to them: 'Do not spread disorder in the land,' they say: 'It is we who reform.' Beware! (Truly) it is they who spread disorder, but they do not have any sense (of it) at all."*
>
> (Al-Qur'an, 11-12)

Here again the mischievous and criminal mentality has been described, and that the offenders never regard their activity as disruption, violence and strife; rather, they may call it Jihad and deeds of reconstruction and reformation. They presume that the tyrannous activities they perpetrate are aimed at the greater good of society. Today's tragedy is that terrorists, murderers, mischief-mongers and rioters try to prove their criminal, rebellious, tyrannous, brutal and blasphemous activities as a right and a justified reaction to foreign aggression under the garb of the defence of Islam and national interests.

They should know that, as good intention can never prove an unlawful act justified, pious designs can never prove blasphemy as righteousness, and virtuous objectives can never prove an impure act wholesome; that the intention to perform Jihad, in the same way, can never prove violence and terrorism lawful and permissible. The intention to protect Islam, to erect a defence against foreign aggression and avenge the wrongs and excesses inflicted upon the Muslim Umma is one thing, but the brutal mass murder of innocent citizens, destruction of civil property, ruthless target killings and the destruction of mosques and markets and businesses is altogether a different debacle. The former can never prove the latter lawful. The one has nothing to do with the other; there is no relevance and congruity between the two. Terrorism, carnage and mass destruction can never be justified in the name of any intention of enforcing Islamic commands and its judicial system. Nor can these reprehensible activities be any exception to the rule, or be overlooked, or forgiven.

An in-depth study of the Qur'an and Hadith makes one resolutely establish that Islam declares the realisation of lawful objectives conditional upon lawful means only, the attainment of noble targets only through permissible ways and reaching sacred objectives by treading only the righteous paths. A sacred goal can never be achieved by following an evil and criminal path. Constructing a mosque, for example, is a pious act, but it cannot be proved lawful to do so by looting a bank. The objectives of mercy cannot be achieved through cruelty and oppression. The designs of an exalted and pious person cannot be materialised by adopting blasphemous methodology. In sum, good cannot be earned by evil means. Fair is fair and foul is foul. It is Satan who says, 'fair is foul and foul is fair.' This is the majesty and purity of the Deen (religion of Islam) that it has purified and reformed both the destination and its path. It has made both objective and method pure and upright.

The people who base their argument on the Hadith, 'actions are judged according to intentions,' in order to justify their brutal ways and cursed means, make false and heretic claims. They cannot set a wrong thing right. This Hadith signifies only those actions that are proven pious, permissible and lawful. Their acceptability has been based on trueness of intention. If the intention is pure, they will be accepted, or else they will be rejected. If the intention is not good, or the coveted intention does not exist, the actions will not be considered acts of worship, despite their apparent righteous value. They will be rejected or discredited. But the actions that are forbidden, unjust, unlawful and blasphemous cannot be made permissible or lawful or just and creditable by even extremely good intentions joined together. This is such a crucial Islamic principle and legal formula that not one of the Companions, pious predecessors, Imams, and authorities of Hadith and exegeses has departed from to date. Some scholars have also interpreted the Hadith, 'actions are judged according to intentions,' as pointing to the expression of deeds according to intentions, that the actions take shape according to the intentions. So a terrorist's actions speak of his intentions. His killings and destructive activities refer to his foul intention and condemnable ideas and beliefs. His heinous actions cannot stem from pious intentions and beliefs. The bloodshed he causes refers only to a cruel man inside him and not any kind and merciful soul. It is, therefore, evident that whatever false implications and foul justifications these rebels, criminals, evil-mongers, tyrannous brutes may put forth to prove their atrocities as acts of Jihad, they have nothing to do with the teachings of Islam.

The Holy Qur'an has vividly described them in this verse:

> *"It is those whose entire struggle is wasted in worldly life, but they presume they are doing very good works."*
>
> (Al-Qur'an, 18: 104)

Bibliography

1. Qur'ān.

Tafsīr al-Qur'ān

2. *Jāmi' al-Bayān,* al-Ṭabarī, Abū Ja'far Muḥammad b. Jarīr b. Yazīd (224-310/839-923). Beirut, Lebanon: Dār al-Fikr, 1405 AH.

3. *Tafsīr al-Qur'ān al-'Azīm*, Ibn Abī Ḥātim, Abū Muḥammad 'Abd al-Raḥmān b. Muḥammad Idrīs al-Rāzī al-Tamīmī (240-327/854-938). Lebanon: al-Maktabat al-'Aṣriyya.

4. *Tafsīr al-Qur'ān al-'Azīm* (generally known as *Ta'wīlāt Ahl al-Sunna),* Māturīdī, Abū Manṣūr Muḥammad b. Muḥammad b. Maḥmūd (d. 333 AH). Beirut, Lebanon: Mu'assisat al-Risāla, 1425/2004 .

5. *Ma'ānī al-Qur'ān al-Karīm,* al-Naḥḥās, Abū Ja'far Aḥmad b. Muḥammad b. Ismā'īl (d. 338 AH). Makka, Saudi Arabia: Jāmi'a Umm al-Qurā, 1409 AH.

6. *Aḥkām al-Qur'ān,* al-Jaṣṣāṣ, Abū Bakr Aḥmad b. 'Alī al-Rāzī (305/370 AH). Beirut, Lebanon: Dār Iḥyā' al-Turāth, 1405 AH.

7. *Baḥr al-'Ulūm* (generally known as *Tafsīr al-Samarkandī),* al-Samarkandī, Abū al-Layth Naṣr b. Muḥammad b. Ibrāhīm al-Ḥanafī (333-373 AH). Beirut, Lebanon: Dār al-Fikr.

8. *Ma'ālim al-Tanzīl,* al-Baghawī, Abū Muḥammad Ḥusayn b. Mas'ūd b. Muḥammad (436-516/1044-1122). Beirut, Lebanon: Dār al-Ma'rifa, 1407/1987.

9. *al-Kashshāf 'an Ḥaqā'iq Ghawāmiḍ al-Tanzīl,* al-Zamakhsharī, Jār Allāh Abū al-Qāsim Maḥmud b. 'Umar (467-538/1075-1144). Beirut, Lebanon: Dār Iḥyā' al-Turāth.

10. *Mafātīḥ al-Ghaib* (generally known as *al-Tafsīr al-Kabīr),* al-Rāzī, Muḥammad b. 'Umar b. Ḥasan b. Ḥusayn b. 'Alī al-Tamīmī (543-606/1149-1210). Beirut, Lebanon: Dār al-Kutub al-'Ilmiyya, 1421 AH.

11. *al-Jāmi' li-Aḥkām al-Qur'ān,* al-Qurṭubī, Abū 'Abd Allāh Muḥammad b. Aḥmad b. Abī Bakr b. Farḥ (d. 671 AH). Cario, Egypt: Dār al-Shu'ab, 1372 AH.

12. *Lubāb al-Ta'wīl fī Ma'ānī al-Tanzīl,* al-Khāzin, 'Alī b. Muḥammad b. Ibrāhīm b. 'Umar b. al-Khalīl (678-741/1279-1340). Beirut, Lebanon: Dār al-Ma'rifa.

13. *Tafsīr al-Qur'ān al-'Aẓīm,* Ibn Kathīr, Abū al-Fidā' Ismā'īl b. 'Umar (701-774/1301-1373). Beirut, Lebanon: Dār al-Fikr, 1401 AH.

14. *al-Lubāb fī 'Ulūm al-Kitāb,* Ibn 'Ādil, Abū Ḥafṣ, Sirāj al-Dīn 'Umar b. 'Alī b. 'Ādil al-Dimashqī, al-Ḥanbalī (d. after 880 AH). Beirut, Lebanon: Dār al-Kutub al-'Ilmiyya, 1419/1998.

15. *Tafsīr al-Jalālayn,* al-Suyūṭī & al-Maḥallī, Jalāl al-Dīn Muḥammad b. Aḥmad al-Maḥallī (d. 864 AH), Jalāl al-Dīn Abū al-Faḍl 'Abd al-Raḥmān b. Abī Bakr b. Muḥammad al-Suyūṭī (849-911/1445-1505). Beirut, Lebanon: Dār ibn Kathīr, 1419-1998.

16. *al-Durr al-Manthūr fī al-Tafsīr bī al-Ma'thūr,* al-Suyūṭī, Jalāl al-Dīn Abū al-Faḍl 'Abd al-Raḥmān b. Abī Bakr b. Muḥammad (849-911/1445-1505). Beirut, Lebanon: Dār al-Fikr, 1993 AD.

17. *al-Tafsīr al-Maẓharī,* al-Qāḍī Thanā' Allāh Pānīpatī (d. 1225/1810). Quetta, Pakistan: Baluchistan Book Depot.

Ḥadīth

18. *al-Ṣaḥīḥ,* al-Bukhārī, Abū 'Abd Allāh Muḥammad b. Ismā'īl b. Ibrāhīm b. al-Mughīra (194-256/810-870). Beirut, Lebanon: Dār Ibn Kathīr, al-Yamāma, 1407/1987.

19. *al-Ṣaḥīḥ,* Muslim, Ibn al-Ḥajjāj b. Muslim b. Ward al-Qushayrī al-Naysābūrī (206-261/821-875). Beirut, Lebanon: Dār Iḥyā' al-Turāth al-'Arabī.

20. *al-Sunan,* al-Tirmidhī, Abū 'Īsā Muḥammad b. 'Īsā b. Sūra b. Mūsā b. al-Ḍaḥḥāk (209-279/825-892). Beirut, Lebanon: Dār Iḥyā' al-Turāth al-'Arabī.

21. *al-Sunan,* al-Nasā'ī, Abū 'Abd al-Raḥmān Aḥmad b. Shu'ayb (215-303/830-915). Beirut, Lebanon: Dār al-Kutub al-'Ilmiyya, 1416/1995 & Ḥalb, Syria: Maktab al-Maṭbū'āt al-Islāmiyya, 1406/1986.

22. *al-Sunan al-Kubrā,* al-Nasā'ī, Abū 'Abd al-Raḥmān Aḥmad b. Shu'ayb (215-303/830-915).

Beirut, Lebanon: Dār al-Kutub al-'Ilmiyya, 1411/1991.

23. *al-Sunan,* Abū Dāwūd, Sulaymān b. al-Ash'ath b. Isḥāq b. Bashīr al-Sijistānī (202-275/817-889). Beirut, Lebanon: Dār al-Fikr, 1414/1994.

24. *al-Sunan,* Ibn Mājah, Abū 'Abd Allāh Muḥammad b. Yazīd al-Qazwīnī (207-275/824-887). Beirut, Lebanon: Dār al-Fikr.

25. *Musnad al-Imām Abī Ḥanīfa,* Abū Nu'aym, Aḥmad b. 'Abd Allāh b. Aḥmad al-Aṣbahānī (336-430/948-1038). Riyadh, Saudi Arabia, Maktabat al-Kawthar, 1415 AH.

26. *al-Muwaṭṭa',* Mālik, Ibn Anas b. Mālik b. Abī 'Amir b. 'Amr b. al-Ḥārith al-Aṣbaḥī (93-179/712-795). Beirut, Lebanon: Dār Iḥyā' al-Turāth al-'Arabī, 1406/1985.

27. *al-Musnad,* al-Shāfi'ī, Abū 'Abd Allāh Muḥammad b. Idrīs b. 'Abbās b. 'Uthmān al-Qurashī (150-204/767-819). Beirut, Lebanon: Dār al-Kutub al-'Ilmiyya.

28. *al-Musnad,* Aḥmad b. Ḥanbal, Abū 'Abd Allāh b. Muḥammad al-Shaybānī (164-241/780-855).

Beirut, Lebanon: al-Maktab al-Islāmī li al-Ṭabā'a wal-Nashr, 1398/1978.

29. *al-Musnad*, Aḥmad b. Ḥanbal, Abū 'Abd Allāh b. Muḥammad al-Shaybānī (164-241/780-855). Beirut, Lebanon: Mu'assisat al-Risāla, 1420/1999.

30. *Faḍā'il al-Ṣaḥāba,* Aḥmad b. Ḥanbal, Abū 'Abd Allāh b. Muḥammad (164-241/780-855). Beirut, Lebanon: Mu'assisat al-Risāla, 1403/1983.

31. *al-Jāmi'*,al-Azdī Ma'mar b. Rāshid, (d. 151 AH). Beirut, Lebanon: al-Maktab al-Islāmī, 1403 AH.

32. *al-Musnad,* al-Ṭayālisī, Abū Dāwūd Sulaymān b. Dāwūd al-Jārūd (133-204/751-819). Beirut, Lebanon: Dār al-Ma'rifa.

33. *al-Muṣannaf,* 'Abd al-Razzāq, Abū Bakr b. Hammām b. al-Nāfi' al-Ṣan'ānī (126-211/744-826). Beirut, Lebanon: al-Maktab al-Islāmī, 1403 AH.

34. *al-Muṣannaf,* Ibn Abī Shayba, Abū Bakr 'Abd Allāh b. Muḥammad (159-235/776-849). Riyadh, Saudi Arabia: Maktabat al-Rushd, 1409 AH.

35. *al-Musnad,* ʻAbd b. Ḥumayd, Abū Muḥammad b. al-Naṣr al-Kasī (d. 249/863). Cairo, Egypt: Maktabat al-Sunna, 1408/1988.

36. *al-Sunan,* al-Dārimī, Abū Muḥammad ʻAbd Allāh b. ʻAbd al-Raḥmān (181-255/797-869). Beirut, Lebanon: Dār al-Kitāb al-ʻArabī, 1407 AH.

37. *al-Sunna,* Ibn Abī ʻĀṣim, Abū Bakr b. ʻAmr al-Ḍaḥḥāk b. Makhlad al-Shaybānī (206-287/822-900). Beirut, Lebanon: al-Maktab al-Islāmī, 1400 AH.

38. *al-Fitan,* Nuʻaym b. Ḥammād, Abū ʻAbd Allāh al-Marwazī (d. 288 AH). Cario, Egypt & Beirut, Lebanon: Mu'assisat al-Kutub al-Thaqāfiyya, 1408 AH.

39. *al-Sunna,* ʻAbd Allāh Ibn Aḥmad, Ibn Muḥammad b. Ḥanbal (213-290 AH). Dammām: Dār Ibn al-Qayyim, 1406 AH.

40. *al-Musnad,* al-Bazzār, Abū Bakr Aḥmad b. ʻAmr b. ʻAbd al-Khāliq al-Baṣrī (215-292/830-905). Beirut, Lebanon: Mu'assisa ʻUlūm al-Qur'ān, 1409 AH.

41. *Musnad Abī Bakr al-Ṣiddiq,* al-Marwazī, Abū Bakr Aḥmad b. ʿAlī b. Saʿīd al-Umawī (d. 202-292 AH). Beirut, Lebanon: al-Maktab al-Islāmī.

42. *al-Musnad,* Abū Yaʿlā, Aḥmad b. ʿAlī b. Mathnā b. Yaḥyā b. ʿĪsā b. Hilāl al-Mūṣilī al-Tamīmī (210-307/825-919). Damascus, Syria: Dār al-Ma'mūn li al-Turāth, 1404/1984.

43. *Musnad al-Ṣaḥāba* (generally known as *Musnad al-Ruyānī),* al-Ruyānī, Abū Bakr Muḥammad b. Hārūn (d. 307 AH). Cairo, Egypt: Mu'assisa Cordoba, 1416 AH.

44. *al-Ṣaḥīḥ,* Ibn Khuzayma, Abū Bakr Muḥammad b. Isḥāq (223-311/838-924). Beirut, Lebanon: al-Maktab al-Islāmī, 1390/1970.

45. *al-Sunna,* al-Khilāl, Abū Bakr Aḥmad b. Muḥammad b. Hārūn b. Yazīd (311-334 AH). Riyadh, Saudi Arabia: Dār al-Rāya, 1410 AH.

46. *al-Musnad,* Abū ʿAwāna, Yaʿqūb b. Isḥāq b. Ibrāhīm b. Zayd al-Naysabūrī (230-316/845-928). Beirut, Lebanon: Dār al-Maʿrifa, 1998 .

47. *al-Muʿjam al-Ṣaghīr,* al-Ṭabarānī, Abū al-Qāsim Sulaymān b. Aḥmad b. Ayyūb b. Maṭīr al-

Lakhmī (260-360/873-970). Beirut, Lebanon: al-Maktab al-Islāmī, 1405/1985.

48. *al-Mu'jam al-Awsaṭ,* al-Ṭabarānī, Abū al-Qāsim Sulaymān b. Aḥmad b. Ayyūb b. Maṭīr al-Lakhmī (260-360/873-970). Cairo, Egypt: Dār al-Ḥaramain, 1415 AH.

49. *al-Mu'jam al-Kabīr,* al-Ṭabarānī, Abū al-Qāsim Sulaymān b. Aḥmad b. Ayyūb b. Maṭīr al-Lakhmī (260-360/873-970). Mosul, Iraq: Maktabat al-'Ulūm wal-Ḥikam, 1403/1983.

50. *Musnad al-Shāmiyyīn,* al-Ṭabarānī, Abū al-Qāsim Sulaymān b. Aḥmad b. Ayyūb b. Maṭīr al-Lakhmī (260-360/873-970). Beirut, Lebanon: Mu'assisat al-Risāla, 1405/1985.

51. *al-Īmān,* Ibn Manda, Abū 'Abd Allāh Muḥammad b. Isḥāq b. Yaḥyā (310-395/922-1005). Beirut, Lebanon: Mu'assisat al-Risāla, 1406 AH.

52. *al-Mustadrak 'alā al-Ṣaḥīḥain,* al-Ḥākim, Abū 'Abd Allāh Muḥammad b. 'Abd Allāh b. Muḥammad (321-405/933-1014). Beirut, Lebanon: Dār al-Kutub al-'Ilmiyya, 1411/1990.

53. *Kitāb al-Arba'īn 'alā Madhhab al-Mutaḥaqqiqīn min al-Ṣufiyya,* Abū Nu'aym, Aḥmad b. 'Abd Allāh b.

Aḥmad b. Isḥāq b. Mūsā b. Mihrān al-Aṣbahānī (336-430/948-1038). Beirut, Lebanon: Dār Ibn Ḥazm, 1414/1993.

54. *al-Sunan al-Kubrā,* al-Bayhaqī, Abū Bakr Aḥmad b. Ḥusayn b. 'Alī b. 'Abd Allāh b. Mūsā (384-458/994-1066). Makka, Saudi Arabia: Maktaba Dār al-Bāz, 1414/1994.

55. *Shu'ab al-Īmān,* al-Bayhaqī, Abū Bakr Aḥmad b. Ḥusayn b. 'Alī b. 'Abd Allāh b. Mūsā (384-458/994-1066). Beirut, Lebanon: Dār al-Kutub al-'Ilmiyya, 1410/1990.

56. *al-Ṣaḥīḥ,* Ibn Ḥibbān, Abū Ḥātim Muḥammad b. Ḥibbān b. Aḥmad b. Ḥibbān (270-354/884-965). Beirut, Lebanon: Mu'assisat al-Risāla, 1414/1993.

57. *al-Sunan,* al-Dāraquṭnī, Abū al-Ḥasan 'Alī b. 'Umar b. Aḥmad b. al-Mahdī b. Mas'ūd b. al-Nu'mān (306-385/918-995). Beirut, Lebanon: Dār al-Ma'rifa, 1386/1966.

58. *Musnad al-Firdaws,* al-Daylamī, Abū Shujā' Shīrawayh b. Shahrdār b. Shīrawayh al-Daylamī al-Hamdānī (445-509/1053-1115). Beirut, Lebanon: Dār al-Kutub al-'Ilmiyya, 1406/1986.

59. *al-Aḥādīth al-Mukhtāra,* al-Maqdisī, Muḥammad b. ʻAbd al-Wāḥid Ḥanbalī, (569-643/1173-1245). Makkah, Saudi Arabia: Maktabat al-Nahḍat al-Ḥadīthiyya, 1410/1990.

60. *al-Targhīb wal-Tarhīb,* al-Mundhirī, Abū Muḥammad ʻAbd al-ʻAzīm b. ʻAbd al-Qawwī b. ʻAbd Allāh b. Salama b. Saʻd (581-656/1185-1258). Beirut, Lebanon: Dār al-Kutub al-ʻIlmiyya, 1417 AH.

61. *Kabā'ir,* al-Dhahabī, Shams al-Dīn Muḥammad b. Aḥmad (673-748/1274-1348). Beirut, Lebanon: Dār al-Nadawat al-Jadīda.

62. *Naṣb al-Rāya lī Aḥadīth al-Hidāya,* al-Zaylaʻī, Abū Muḥammad ʻAbd Allāh b. Yūsuf al-Ḥanafī (d. 762/1360). Egypt: Dār al-Ḥadīth, 1357/1938.

63. *Jāmiʻ al-ʻUlūm wal-Ḥikam fī Sharḥ Khamsīn Ḥadīan min Jawāmiʻ al-Kalim,* Ibn Rajab al-Ḥanbalī, Abū al-Faraj ʻAbd al-Raḥmān b. Aḥmad (736-795 AH). Beirut, Lebanon: Dār al-Maʻrifa, 1408 AH.

64. *Majmaʻ al-Zawā'id,* al-Haythamī, Nūr al-Dīn Abū al-Ḥasan ʻAlī b. Abī Bakr b. Sulaymān (735-807/1335-1405). Cairo, Egypt: Dār al-

Riyān lī al-Turāth & Beirut Lebanon: Dār al-Kitab al-'Arabī, 1407/1987.

65. *al-Dirāya fī Takhrīj Aḥādīth al-Hidāya*, Ibn Ḥajar al-'Asqalānī, Aḥmad b. 'Alī b. Muḥammad b. Muḥammad b. 'Alī b. Aḥmad al-Kinānī (773-852/1372-1449). Beirut, Lebanon, Dār al-Ma'rifa.

66. *Hady al-Sārī Muqqadima Fatḥ al-Bārī*, Ibn Ḥajar al-'Asqalānī, Aḥmad b. 'Alī b. Muḥammad b. Muḥammad b. 'Alī b. Aḥmad al-Kinānī (773-852/1372-1449). Beirut, Lebanon, Dār al-Ma'rifa.

67. *al-Jāmi' al-Ṣaḥīḥ - Musnad al-Imām al-Rabī' b. Ḥabīb*, al-Azdī, Rabī' b. Ḥabīb b. 'Umar al-Baṣrī (95-153/713-770). Beirut, Lebanon: Dār al-Ḥikma, 1415 AH.

68. *Kanz al-'Ummāl fī Sunan al-Aqwāl wal-Af'āl*, Ḥussam al-Dīn al-Hindī, 'Alā' al-Dīn 'Alī al-Muttaqī (d. 975 AH). Beirut, Lebanon: Mu'assisat al-Risāla, 1399/1979.

69. *Ash'at al-Lam'āt Sharḥ Mishkāt al-Maṣābīḥ*, 'Abd al-Ḥaqq, Muḥaddith al-Dihlawī (958-1052/1551-1642). Sakhar, Pakistan, Maktaba Nūriyya Riḍwiyya, 1976 AD.

70. *Kashf al-Khifā' wā Muzīl al-Ilbās,* al-'Ajlūnī, Abū al-Fidā' Ismā'īl b. Muḥammad al-Jarrāḥī (1087-1162/1676-1749). Beirut, Lebanon: Mu'assisat al-Risāla, 1405/1985.

71. *Silsilat al-Aḥādīth al-Ṣaḥīḥa,* al-Albānī, Muḥammad Nāṣir al-Dīn (1333-1420/1914-1999). Beirut, Lebanon: al-Maktab al-Islāmī, 1405/1985.

Ḥadīth Commentaries

72. *Sharḥ Ṣaḥīḥ al-Bukhārī,* Ibn Baṭṭāl, Abū al-Ḥasan 'Alī b. Khalf b. 'Abd al-Malik b. Baṭṭāl al-Qurṭubī (d. 449 AH). Riyadh, Saudi Arabia: Maktabat al-Rushd, 1423/2003.

73. *al-Tamhīd,* Ibn 'Abd al-Barr, Abū 'Umar Yūsuf b. 'Abd Allāh (368-463/979-1071). Morocco: Wazārat 'Umūm al-Awqāf, 1387 AH.

74. *Ikmāl al-Mu'lim bi-Fawā'id Muslim,* al-Qāḍī 'Iyāḍ, Abū al-Faḍl 'Iyāḍ b. Mūsā b. 'Iyāḍ b. 'Amr b. Mūsā al-Yaḥṣubī (476-544/1083-1149). Beirut, Lebanon: Dār al-Wafā li al-Ṭabā'a wal-Nashr wal-Tawzī', 1419/1998.

75. *al-Mufhim Limā Ushkila min Talkḥīṣ Kitāb Muslim,* Abū al-'Abbās al-Qurṭubī, Aḥmad b.

'Umar b. Ibrāhīm (578-656 AH). Beirut, Lebanon & Damascus, Syria: Dār Ibn Kathīr, 1420/1999.

76. *Sharḥ al-Nawawī 'alā Ṣaḥīḥ Muslim,* al-Nawawī, Abū Zakariyyā Yaḥyā b. Sharaf b. al-Murrī (631-676). Beirut, Labanon: Dār Iḥyā' al-Turāth, 1392 AH.

77. *Fatḥ al-Bārī Sharḥ Ṣaḥīḥ al-Bukarī,* Ibn Ḥajar al-'Asqalānī, Aḥmad b. 'Alī b. Muḥammad b. Muḥammad b. 'Alī b. Aḥmad al-Kinānī (773-852/1372-1449). Beirut, Lebanon, Dār al-Ma'rifa, 1379 AH.

78. *'Umdat al-Qārī Sharḥ 'alā Ṣaḥīḥ al-Bukhārī,* al-'Aynī, Badr al-Dīn Abū Muḥammad Maḥmūd b. Aḥmad b. Mūsā b. Aḥmad b. al-Ḥusayn b. Yūsuf b. Maḥmūd (762-855/1361-1451). Beirut, Lebanon: Dār Iḥyā' al-Turāth al-'Arabī.

79. *Irshād al-Sārī li-Sharḥ Ṣaḥīḥ al-Bukhārī,* al-Qasṭalānī, Abū al-'Abbās Aḥmad b. Muḥammad b. Abī Bakr b. 'Abd al-Mālik b. Aḥmad b. Muḥammad b. Muḥammad b. al-Ḥusayn b. 'Alī (851-923/1448-1517). Beirut, Lebanon: Dār al-Fikr.

80. *Mirqāt al-Mafātiḥ Sharḥ Mishkāt al-Maṣābīḥ*, Mullā 'Alī al-Qārī, 'Alī b. Sulṭān Muḥammad Nūr al-Dīn al-Ḥanafī (d. 1014/1606). Multan, Pakistan: Maktaba Imdādiyya.

81. *Fayḍ al-Qadīr Sharḥ al-Jāmi' al-Ṣaghīr*, al-Manāwī, 'Abd al-Rawf b. Tāj al-Ārifīn b. 'Alī b. Zayn al-'Abidīn (952-1031/1545-1621). Egypt: Maktabat al-Tajjāriyyat al-Kubrā, 1356 AH.

82. *Tuḥfat al-Aḥwadhī fī Sharḥ Jāmi' al-Tirmidhī*, al-Mubārakfūrī, Muḥammad 'Abd al-Raḥmān b. 'Abd al-Raḥīm (1283-1353 AH). Beirut, Lebanon: Dār al-Kutub al-'Ilmiyya.

83. *Fatḥ al-Mulhim bi-Sharḥ Ṣaḥīḥ al-Imām Muslim*, Shabbīr Aḥmad al-Uthmānī, Ibn Faḍl al-Raḥmān al-Hindī (1305-1369/1889-1949). Damascus, Syria: Dār al-Qalam, 1427/2006.

Asmā' al-Rijāl

84. *al-Tārīkh al-Kabīr*, al-Bukhārī, Abū 'Abd Allāh Muḥammad b. Ismā'īl b. Ibrāhīm b. al-Mughīra (194-256/810-870). Beirut, Lebanon: Dār al-Kutub al-'Ilmiyya, 1422/2001.

85. *Siyar A'lām al-Nubalā'*, al-Dhahabī, Shams al-Dīn Muḥammad b. Aḥmad (673-748/1274-

1348). Beirut, Lebanon: Mu'assisat al-Risāla, 1413 AH.

86. *Tahdhīb al-Tahdhīb,* Ibn Ḥajar al-'Asqalānī, Aḥmad b. 'Alī b. Muḥammad b. Muḥammad b. 'Alī b. Aḥmad al-Kinānī (773-852/1372-1449). Beirut, Lebanon: Dār al-Fikr, 1404/1984.

87. *al-Iṣāba fī Tamyīz al-Ṣahāba,* Ibn Ḥajar al-'Asqalānī, Aḥmad b. 'Alī b. Muḥammad b. Muḥammad b. 'Alī b. Aḥmad al-Kinānī (773-852/1372-1449). Beirut, Lebanon: Dār al-Jīl, 1412/1993.

Fiqh and Uṣūl al-Fiqh

88. *al-Mudawwanat al-Kubrā,* Mālik, Ibn Anas b. Mālik b. Abī 'Amir b. 'Amr b. al-Ḥārith al-Aṣbaḥī (93-179/712-795). Beirut, Lebanon: Dār al-Ṣādir.

89. *Kitāb al-Kharāj,* Abū Yūsuf, Ya'qūb b. Ibrāhīm (113/731-182/798). Beirut, Lebanon: Dār al-Ma'rifa.

90. *al-Aṣl* (generally known as *al-Mabsūṭ),* al-Shaybanī, Abū 'Abd Allāh Muḥammad b. al-Ḥasan b. Farqad (132-189 AH). Karachi,

Pakistan: Idārat al-Qur'ān wal-'Ulūm al-Islāmiyya.

91. *Kitāb al-Ḥujja 'alā Ahl al-Madīna,* al-Shaybanī, Abū 'Abd Allāh Muḥammad b. al-Ḥasan b. Farqad (132-189 AH). Beirut, Lebanon: 'Ālam al-Kutub, 1403 AH.

92. *Kitāb al-Kharāj,* Yaḥyā b. Ādam, Abū Zakariyya b. Sulaymān al-Qurashī (d. 203 AH). Lahore, Pakistan: al-Maktabat al-Islāmiyya, 1974 AD.

93. *al-Umm,* al-Shāfi'ī, Abū 'Abd Allāh Muḥammad b. Idrīs b. 'Abbās b. 'Uthmān b. Shāfi' al-Qurashī (150-204/767-819). Beirut, Lebanon: Dār al-Ma'rifa, 1393 AH.

94. *Kitāb al-Amwāl,* Abū 'Ubayd, al-Qāsim b. al-Salām (d. 224 AH). Beirut, Lebanon: Dār al-Fikr, 1408 AH.

95. *Kitāb al-Amwāl,* Ibn Zanjawaih, Ḥumayd (251 AH). Riyadh, Saudi Arabia: Markaz al-Malik Faisal li al-Baḥuth wal-Dirasāt al-Islāmiyya, 1406/1986.

96. *al-Diyāt,* Ibn Abī 'Āṣim, Abū Bakr 'Amr al-Ḍaḥḥāk al-Shaybānī (206-287/822-900).

Karachi, Pakistan: Idārat al-Qur'ān wal-'Ulūm, 1407 AH.

97. *Ta'ẓīm Qadr al-Ṣalāt,* al-Marwazī, Abū 'Abd Allāh Muḥammad b. Naṣr b. al-Ḥajjāj (202-294 AH). Madina, Saudi Arabia, Maktabat al-Dār, 1406 AH.

98. *Sharḥ Ma'ānī al-Āthār,* al-Ṭaḥāwī, Abū Ja'far Aḥmad b. Muḥammad b. Salama (229-321/853-933). Beirut, Lebanon: Dār al-Kutub al-'Ilmiyya, 1399 AH.

99. *Mukhtaṣar al-Kharaqī min Masā'il al-Imām Aḥmad b. Ḥanbal,* al-Kharaqī, Abū al-Qāsim 'Umar b. Ḥusayn (d. 334 AH). Beirut, Lebanon: al-Maktab al-Islāmī, 1403 AH.

100. *al-Aḥkām al-Sulṭāniyya,* al-Māwardī, Abū al-Ḥasan 'Alī b. Muḥammad b. Ḥabīb al-Baṣrī (364-450 AH). Beirut, Lebanon: Dār al-Kutub al-'Ilmiyya, 1398/1978.

101. *al-Iqnā' fī al-Fiqh al-Shāfi'ī,* al-Māwardī, Abū al-Ḥasan 'Alī b. Muḥammad b. Ḥabīb al-Baṣrī (d. 364-450 AH).

102. *al-Muḥallā,* Ibn Ḥazm, 'Alī b. Aḥmad b. Sa'īd b. Ḥazm al-Andalusī (383-456/993-1064). Beirut, Lebanon: Dār al-Āfāq al-Jadīda.

103. *al-Kāfī fī Fiqh Ahl al-Madīna,* Ibn 'Abd al-Barr, Abū 'Umar Yūsuf b. 'Abd Allāh b. Muḥammad (368-463/979-1071). Beirut, Lebanon: Dār al-Kutub al-'Ilmiyya, 1407 AH.

104. *Kitāb al-Mabsūṭ,* al-Sarkhasī, Shams al-Dīn (d. 483 AH). Beirut, Lebanon: Dār al-Ma'rifa, 1398/1978.

105. *al-Mu'talif min al-Mukhtalif baina Ā'imma al-Salaf,* al-Ṭabrasī, Abū 'Alī al-Faḍl b. al-Ḥasan (d. 548 AH). Qom, Iran, Maṭba'a Sayyid al-Shuhadā', 1410 AH.

106. *al-Ifṣāḥ 'an Ma'ānī al-Ṣiḥaḥ fī al-Fiqh 'alā al-Madhāhib al-Arba'a,* Ibn Habīrah, Wazīr Abū al-Muẓaffar 'Awn al-Dīn Yaḥyā b. Habīrah al-Ḥanbalī (d. 560 AH).

107. *Badā'i' al-Ṣanā'i',* al-Kāsānī, 'Alā' al-Dīn (d. 587 AH). Beirut, Lebanon: Dār al-Kitab al-'Arabī, 1982 AD.

108. *al-Hidāya Sharḥ al-Bidāya,* al-Murghaynānī, Abū al-Ḥasan 'Alī b. Abī Bakr b. 'Abd al-Jalīl (511-593 AH). Beirut, Lebanon: al-Maktabat al-Islāmiyya.

109. *Bidāyat al-Mujtahid,* Ibn Rushd, Abū al-Walīd Muḥammad b. Aḥmad b. Muḥammad b. Rushd

al-Qurṭubī (d. 595 AH). Beirut, Lebanon: Dār al-Fikr.

110. *al-Kāfī fī Fiqh b. Ḥanbal,* Ibn Qudāma, Abū Muḥammad 'Abd Allāh b. Aḥmad al-Maqdisī (541-620). Beirut, Lebanon: al-Maktab al-Islāmī.

111. *al-Mughnī fī Fiqh al-Imām Aḥmad b. Ḥanbal al-Shaybānī,* Ibn Qudāma, Abū Muḥammad 'Abd Allāh b. Aḥmad al-Maqdisī (541-620 AH). Beirut, Lebanon: Dār al-Fikr, 1405 AH.

112. *Rawḍat al-Ṭālibīn wā 'Umdat al-Muftīn,* al-Nawawī, Abū Zakariyyā Yaḥyā b. Sharaf (631-676). Beirut, Labanon: al-Maktab al-Islāmī, 1405 AH.

113. *al-Dhakhīra fī al-Fiqh al-Mālikī,* al-Qarāfī, Abū al-'Abbās Shihāb al-Dīn Aḥmad b. Idrīs al-Mālikī (d. 684 AH). Beirut, Lebanon: Dār al-Gharb, 1994 AD.

114. *Anwār al-Barūq fī Anwā' al-Furūq,* al-Qarāfī, Abū al-'Abbās al-Shihāb al-Dīn Aḥmad b. Idrīs al-Mālikī (d. 684 AH). Beirut, Lebanon: Dār al-Kutub al-'Ilmiyya, 1418/1998.

115. *al-Qawanīn al-Fiqhiyya,* Ibn al-Jazarī, Muḥammad b. Aḥmad b. al-Jazarī al-Kalbī al-Gharnāṭī (693-741 AH).

116. *Aḥkām Ahl al-Dhimma,* Ibn al-Qayyim, Abū 'Abd Allāh Muḥammad b. Abī Bakr Ayyūb al-Zar'ī (691-751/1292-1350). Beirut, Lebanon: Dār Ibn Ḥazm, 1418/1997.

117. *al-Furū',* Ibn Mufliḥ, Abū 'Abd Allāh Shams al-Dīn al-Maqdisī al-Ḥanbalī (717-762 AH). Beirut, Lebanon: Dār al-Kutub al-'Ilmiyya, 1418.

118. *al-I'tiṣām,* al-Shāṭibī, Abū Isḥāq Ibrāhīm b. Mūsā b. Muḥammad al-Gharnaṭī (d. 790 AH). Egypt: al-Maktabat al-Tujjariyya.

119. *Fatḥ al-Qadīr Sharḥ al-Hidāya,* Ibn Hammām, Kamāl al-Dīn Muḥammad b. 'Abd al-Wāḥid al-Siwāsī al-Sikandarī (790-861 AH). Quetta, Pakistan: Maktabat al-Rashīdiyya.

120. *al-Bināya Sharḥ al-Hidāya,* al-'Aynī, Badr al-Dīn Abū Muḥammad Maḥmūd b. Aḥmad b. Mūsā b. Aḥmad b. al-Ḥusayn b. Yūsuf b. Maḥmūd (762-855/1361-1451).

121. *al-Mubdi‘ fī Sharḥ al-Muqni‘*, Ibn Mufliḥ, Abū Isḥāq Ibrāhīm b. Muḥammad, b. ‘Abd Allāh al-Ḥanbalī (816/884 AH). Beirut, Lebanon: al-Maktab al-Islāmī.

122. *al-Inṣāf fī Ma‘rifat al-Rājiḥ min al-Khilāf ‘alā Madhhab al-Imām Aḥmad b. Hanbal*, al-Mardāwī, Abū al-Ḥasan ‘Alā’ al-Dīn ‘Alī b. Sulaymān b. Aḥmad b. Muḥammad (d. 817-885 AH). Beirut, Lebanon: Dār Iḥyā’ al-Turāh al-‘Arabī.

123. *Manhaj al-Ṭullāb*, Zakariyya al-Anṣārī, Abū Yaḥyā b. Muḥammad b. Aḥmad (823-926 AH). Beirut, Lebanon: Dār al-Kutub al-‘Ilmiyya, 1418 AH.

124. *al-Baḥr al-Rā’iq Sharḥ Kanz al-Daqā’iq*, Ibn Nujaym, Zayn b. Ibrāhīm b. Muḥammad b. Muḥammad b. Muḥammad b. Bakr al-Ḥanafī (926-970 AH). Beirut, Lebanon: Dār al-Ma‘rifa.

125. *al-Iqnā‘ fī Ḥall Alfāẓ Abī Shujā‘*, al-Sharbīnī, Muḥammad al-Khaṭīb (d. 977 AH). Beirut, Lebanon: Dār al-Fikr, 1415 AH.

126. *Mughnī al-Muḥtāj ilā Ma‘rifa Ma‘ānī Alfāẓ al-Minhāj*, al-Sharbīnī, Muḥammad al-Khaṭīb (d. 977 AH). Beirut, Lebanon: Dār Iḥyā’ al-Turāth al-‘Arabī, 1402/1982.

127. *Ghāyat al-Muntahī*, Mar'ī, Ibn Yūsuf b. Abī Bakr b. Aḥmad Karmī al-Maqdisī al-Ḥanbalī (d. 1033 AH).

128. *Kashshāf al-Qinā' 'an Matn al-'Iqnā*, Buhūtī, Manṣūr b. Yūnus b. Idrīs (1000-1051/1591-1641). Beirut, Lebanon: Dār al-Fikr, 1402 AH.

129. *Al-Durr al-Mukhtār fī Sharḥ Tanwīr al-Abṣār*, al-Ḥaṣkafī, Muḥammad 'Alā al-Dīn b. 'Alī al-Ḥanafī (1025-1088 AH). Beirut Lebanon: Dār al-Fikr, 1386 AH.

130. *Ḥāshiyat al-Bujairmī 'alā Sharḥ Manhaj al-Ṭūllāb*, al-Bujayrmī, Sulaymān b. 'Umar b. Muḥammad. Diyār Bakr: Turkey: al-Makatabat al-Islāmiyya.

131. *Nayl al-Awṭār Sharḥ Muntaqā al-Akhbār*, al-Shawkānī, Muḥammad b. 'Alī b. Muḥammad (d. 1255 AH). Beirut, Lebanon: Dār al-Jīl, 1973 AD.

132. *Ḥāshiyat al-Dusūqī 'alā Sharḥ al-Kabīr*, al-Dusūqī, Muḥammad b. Aḥmad al-'Arafa al-Mālikī (1230/1815 AH). Beirut, Lebanon: Dār al-Fikr.

133. *Radd al-Mukhtār 'alā al-Durr al-Mukhtār 'alā Tanwīr al-Abṣār*, Ibn 'Ābidīn al-Shāmī,

Muḥammad b. Muḥammad Amīn b. ʻUmar b. ʻAbd al-ʻAzīz ʻĀbidīn al-Dimashqī (1244-1306 AH). Beirut, Lebanon: Dār al-Fikr, 1386 AH.

134. *al-Sharḥ al-Kabīr,* al-Dardīr, Abū al-Barakāt Aḥmad, Beirut, Lebanon: Dār al-Fikr.

135. *al-Fiqh ʻalā al-Madhāhib al-ʻArbaʻa,* ʻAbd al-Raḥmān al-Jazīrī, Beirut, Lebanon: Dār Iḥyā' al-Turāth al-ʻArabī.

136. *Maṭālib Ūlī al-Nahy,* Muṣṭafā b. Saʻd, Damascus, Syria: al-Maktab al-Islāmī, 1961.

137. *al-Jihād wā Ḍawābiṭat al-Sharʻiyya,* Fawzān, Ṣāliḥ b. Fawzān b. ʻAbd Allāh.

Sīra

138. *al-Ṭabaqāt al-Kubrā,* Ibn Saʻd, Abū ʻAbd Allāh Muḥammad (168-230/784-845). Beirut, Lebanon: Dār Beirut lī al-Ṭabat wal-Nashr, 1398/1978.

139. *al-Shifā bi-Taʻrīf Ḥuqūq al-Muṣṭafā,* al-Qāḍī ʻIyāḍ, Abū al-Faḍl ʻIyāḍ b. Mūsā b. ʻIyāḍ b. ʻAmr b. Mūsā al-Yaḥṣubī (476-544/1083-1149). Beirut, Lebanon: Dār al-Kitab al-ʻArabī.

'Aqā'id

140. *al-Fiqh al-Absaṭ (Majmū'at al-'Aqīda wa 'Ilm al-Kalām li al-Shaykh Zāhid al-Kawthrī).* Abū Ḥanīfa, al-Imām al-A'ẓam al-Nu'mān b. Thābit (80-150 AH). Beirut, Lebanon: Dār al-Kutub al-'Ilmiyya, 1425/2004.

141. *al-'Aqīdat al-Ṭaḥāwiyya,* al-Ṭaḥāwī, Abū Ja'far Aḥmad b. Muḥammad b. Salama (229-321/853-933). Beirut, Lebanon: Dār al-Kutub al-'Ilmiyya, 1399 AH.

142. *al-Sharī'a*, al-Ājurī, Abū Bakr Muḥammad b. al-Ḥusayn b. 'Abd Allāh (d. 360 AH). Riyadh, Saudi Arabia: Dār al-Waṭn, 1420, 1999.

143. *al-Milal wal-Niḥal,* al-Shahristānī, Abū al-Fatḥ Muḥammad b. 'Abd al-Karīm b. Abī Bakr Aḥmad (479-548 AH). Beirut, Lebanon: Dār al-Ma'rifa, 2001 AH.

144. *al-Nubuwwāt,* Ibn Taymiyya, Aḥmad b. 'Abd al-Ḥalīm al-Ḥarānī (661-728/1263-1328). Beirut, Lebanon: Dār al-Kitab al-'Arabī, 1405/1985.

145. *Sharḥ al-'Aqīdat al-Ṭaḥawiyya,* Ibn Abī al-'Izz, Ṣadr al-Dīn Muḥammad b. 'Alā al-Dīn al-Ḥanafī (d. 731-792 AH). Beirut, Lebanon: al-Maktab al-Islāmī, 1408/1988.

146. *al-Faraq bayn al-Firaq wā Bayān al-Firqa al-Nājīyya*, 'Abd al-Qāhir Baghdādī, Abū Manṣūr b. Ṭāhir b. Muḥammad (d. 429-1037). Beirut, Lebanon: Dār al-Āfāq al-Jadīda, 1977 AD.

147. *Tuḥfat Ithnā 'Ashariyya*, 'Abd al-'Azīz al-Muḥaddith al-Dihlawī, (d. 1239/1823). Istanbul, Turkey: Maktabat al-Ḥaqīqa, 1408/1988.

Fatāwā

148. *Majmū' Fatāwā*, Ibn Taymiyya, Aḥmad b. 'Abd al-Ḥalīm al-Ḥarānī (661-728/1263-1328). Maktaba Ibn Taymiyya.

149. *al-Fatāwā al-Tātārkhāniyya fī al-Fiqh al-Ḥanafī*, Ibn 'Alā', 'Ālim b. al-'Alā' al-Anṣārī al-Ḥanafī al-Dihlawī (d. 786 AH). Beirut, Lebanon: Dār al-Kutub al-'Ilmiyya, 2005 AD.

150. *al-Fatāwā al-Bazzāziyya 'alā Hāmish al-Fatāwā al-'Ālamghīriyya*, Ibn al-Bazzāz, Muḥammad b. Muḥammad b. Shihāb al-Kardarī (d. 827 AH). Beirut, Lebanon: Dār al-Ma'rifa, 1393/1973.

151. *Fatāwā Nadhīriyya*, Nadhīr Ḥusayn, Sayyid al-Dihlawī (1800-1903 AD), Gujranwala, Pakistan, Maktabat al-Ma'ārif al-Islāmiyya, 1409/1988.

152. *al-'Aṭāyā al-Nabawiyya fī al-Fatāwā al-Raḍawiyya,* Aḥmad Raḍā, Ibn Naqī 'Alī Khān al-Qādrī (1272-1340/1856-1921). Lahore, Pakistan: Raḍā Foundation, Jāmi'a al-Niẓmiyya al-Raḍawiyya, 1991 AD.

153. *al-Fatāwā al-Shar'iyya fī al-Qaḍāyā al-'Aṣriyya,* Fahad al-Ḥuṣain.

Tasawwuf

154. *al-Ahwāl,* Ibn Abī al-Dunyā, Abū Bakr 'Abd Allāh b. Muḥammad b. al-Qurashī (208-281 AH).

155. *Ḥilyat al-Awliyā' wā Tabaqāt al-Aṣfiyā',* Abū Nu'aym, Aḥmad b. 'Abd Allāh b. Aḥmad b. Isḥāq b. Mūsā b. Mihrān al-Aṣbahānī (336-430/948-1038). Beirut, Lebanon: Dār al-Kitāb al-'Arabī, 1405/1985.

History

156. *Futuḥ al-Buldān,* Balādhurī, Aḥmad b. Yaḥyā b. Jābir (d. 279 AH). Beirut, Lebanon: Dār al-Kutub al-'Ilmiyya, 1403/1983.

157. *Tārīkh al-Umam wal-Mulūk,* al-Ṭabarī, Abū Ja'far Muḥammad b. Jarīr b. Yazīd (224-

310/839-923). Beirut, Lebanon: Dār al-Kutub al-'Ilmiyya, 1407 AH.

158. *al-Iqtiṣād al-Hādī ilā Ṭarīq al-Rishād,* al-Ṭūsī, Abū Ja'far Muḥammad b. Ḥasan (385/460 AH). Tehran, Iran: Maktabat Jāmi' Chehalsatūn.

159. *Tārīkh Baghdād,* al-Khaṭīb al-Baghdādī, Abū Bakr Aḥmad b. 'Alī b. Thābit b. Aḥmad (393-463/1003-1071). Beirut, Lebanon: Dār al Kutāb al-'Ilmiyya.

160. *Tārīkh Dimashq al-Kabīr* (generally known as *Tārīkh Ibn 'Asākīr),* Ibn 'Asākir, Abū al-Qāsim 'Alī b. al-Ḥasan b. Hibat Allāh b. 'Abd Allāh b. al-Ḥusayn al-Dimashqī (499-571/1105-1176). Beirut, Lebanon: Dār al-Fikr, 1995 AD.

161. *al-Kāmil fī al-Tārīkh,* Ibn al-Athīr, Abū al-Ḥasan 'Alī b. Muḥammad b. 'Abd al-Karīm al-Shaybānī al-Jazarī (555-630/1160-1233). Beirut, Lebanon: Dār al-Ṣādir, 1399/1979.

162. *al-Bidāya wal-Nihāya (al-Sīra),* Ibn Kathīr, Abū al-Fidā' Ismā'īl b. 'Umar (701-774/1301-1373). Beirut, Lebanon: Maktabat al-Ma'ārif.

163. *Muqaddima,* Ibn Khaldūn, ʻAbd al-Raḥmān b. Muḥammad al-Ḥaḍramī (732-808 AH). Beirut, Lebanon: Dār al-Qalam, 1984 AD.

Dictionaries

164. *Tahdhīb al-Lugha,* al-Azharī, Abū Manṣūr Muḥammad b. Aḥmad (282-370 AH).

165. *Muʻjam Maqāīs al-Lugha,* Ibn Fāris, Abū al-Ḥusayn Aḥmad b. Fāris b. Zakariyya al-Qazwīnī al-Rāzī (d. 395 AH). Damascus, Syria: Ittiḥād al-Kitāb al-ʻArab, 1423/2002.

166. *al-Nihāya fī Gharīb al-Athar,* al-Jazarī, Abū al-Sʻādāt al-Mubarak b. Muḥammad (544-606 AH). Beirut, Lebanon: al-Maktabat al-ʻIlmiyya, 1399 AH.

167. *Lisān al-ʻArab,* Ibn Manẓūr, Muḥammad b. Mukarram (630-711/1232-1311). Beirut, Lebanon: Dār Ṣādir.

Miscellaneous

168. *Mabādī al-Islām wā Manhaju-hū,* Ismāʻīl Muḥammad Mayqā (164-241/780-855).

169. *al-Muslimūn wal-Islām,* 'Abduh, Muḥammad (1265-1323/1849-1905).

170. www.binbaz.org.sa/mat/1934

Books in English

171. *History of the Arabs,* Hitti, Philip K., Macmilan Education Ltd., 1991.

172. *Islamic Political Thought,* Watt, Montgomery Watt, Edinburgh University Press, 1980.

NOTES

NOTES

NOTES

NOTES